Praise Him In The Dance

By

Marvelous Dance Ministries - Regina S. Wright

authorHOUSE™

1663 LIBERTY DRIVE, SUITE 200
BLOOMINGTON, INDIANA 47403
(800) 839-8640
WWW.AUTHORHOUSE.COM

First published by AuthorHouse 03/08/05

ISBN: 1-4208-0462-6 (sc)

Printed in the United States of America
Bloomington, Indiana

This book is printed on acid-free paper.

Dedication

I dedicate this book to my family.

To Robert, my wonderful husband, who is an awesome example of how a man is to love his wife. If I had to describe you in two words, it would be "my covering." To my sons, Darren and Andrew, your obedience to God has made raising you easy. You guys have always loved and supported Mommy and it has meant all the world to me. To my daughter, Donya, my little cheerleader, it has been a pleasure watching someone other than myself excited about what God is doing in my life. I love you all so very much.

Acknowledgments

To Jesus Christ, the one I always look to for my help. Without you, I am nothing.

To AuthorHouse Publishers, for giving me the opportunity to share my passion with the world.

To Evangelist Ericka McKnight for your words of encouragement.

To Marlene for having a listening ear and for keeping me focused.

Introduction

*D*ance is one of the most important expressions of praise, worship, and thanksgiving to our God. It is also a reminder to the devil that he is defeated in our lives. Dance is a physical way of dealing with the things we are going through spiritually. Praying and singing are not always enough. Sometimes it takes praying, singing, and dancing before God to break through demonic forces the enemy sets before us. Many of the victories in my life came as a result of dancing before God. When faced with a dilemma, whether it's physically, financially, or even spiritually, I've learned that my breakthrough is in my praise, and as I offer my praise before the Lord in the dance, He in return puts demons to flight and gives me peace in whatever I am facing. Many times, He gives me the wisdom and knowledge of how to handle the dilemma.

Throughout the Bible, there are accounts of God's people dancing before Him. The men and women, young and old, all worshipped God in the dance. Dance was very much a part of the Jewish culture. They danced for victories in battle, to offer praise and thanksgiving for the harvest, and even to welcome family or guests to their homes. Dance was without question an essential part of their worship unto God.

Marvelous Dance Ministries is a ministry called by God to restore biblical dance to the body of Christ. Our primary purpose is to assist congregations with the establishment of liturgical dance ministries. I have the privilege of ministering in the dance at churches of all denominations, and I find that in many churches, dance is a form of entertainment and not an integral part of worship. The dance ministries in the church today for the most part consist of members who joined the ministry for every reason imagined except for what God intended. For reasons such as to lose weight or because they were great dancers in the world; surely they must be called to the ministry of dance, and the biggest of all is to be seen by man.

Everyone is commanded to dance, but everyone is not called to the ministry of dance. There is a difference. The people who are commanded to dance are the ones God is referring to in Psalms 150:4. This is the congregation as a whole praising and worshipping God in the dance for His mighty works and according to His excellent greatness. This does not require skill, it only requires obedience. The people who are called to the ministry of dance are anointed by God, with the ability to skillfully bring the words of a song to life through expressive movements and to prepare the heart of man to receive the word of God. Without this anointing, the person is merely doing dance movements and therefore burdens are not removed and yokes are not destroyed in the lives of the people.

Churches can assure that they have people in the ministry who are called by God by first appointing a leader over the dance ministry. This should be someone whom God revealed to the leader of the church in prayer. Secondly, conduct an audition. The audition will give the dance leader the opportunity to see the skill and character of the people auditioning. The dance ministry should consist of praise dancers who are skillful in the dance. However, there are people who are called to the ministry of dance with great potential and need to develop their skill through training. God will reveal those people to the dance leader during the auditions. Although technical skill is important, the praise dancer must understand that their main purpose is to present their bodies as living sacrifices to God so that through them, He may be glorified in the lives of the people on earth. A praise dancer must live a life that is holy and acceptable to

God. The fruit of the Spirit, love, joy, peace, longsuffering, gentleness, goodness, faith, meekness, and temperance should be the characteristics of a praise dancer.

The function of the dance in the church is twofold. The primary function is for the congregation to praise and worship God. The other function is of the dance ministry as part of the praise team during praise and worship. While searching the scriptures, I found some reasons why the people of God danced, and compiled them in this book, along with some of my personal experiences of dancing before God. I pray that it causes a spirit of dance to rise up within you, and that you make dance a part of your worship at home and at church. I'm sure you will be able to identify an area in your life where you need to put dance. So let us find our rightful place in the dance, whether it's in the dance ministry or in the congregation. Let us praise and worship the Lord of the dance, Jesus Christ. He is worthy, isn't He?

Table of Contents

Created by Him and for Him

"For by Him were all things created, that are in heaven, and that are in the earth, visible and invisible, whether they be by thrones, or dominions, or principalities or powers: ALL THINGS WERE CREATED BY HIM AND FOR HIM." (Colossians 1:16)

"And it came to pass, as soon as he came high unto the camp, that he saw the calf, and DANCING: and Moses' anger waxed hot, and he cast the tables out of his hands and brake them beneath the mount." (Exodus 32:19)

"But when Herod's birthday was kept, the daughter of Herodias DANCED before them, and pleased Herod." (Matthew 14:6)

Although dance is the Lord's doing and marvelous in our eyes, it is not for our entertainment. It was created by God and for

1

God. My pastor says in most of her messages that "God will not share His glory with anyone. He will allow us to enjoy it, but we must give all the glory to Him." Any expression of dance outside of pleasing God, glorifies man. There is no in- between. It either glorifies God or it doesn't.

There are two accounts of dance recorded in the Bible that did not give God glory. In *Exodus 32:19,* the Israelites were worshipping a man-made god in the dance, and in *Matthew 14:6,* the daughters of Herodias were dancing lustfully before Herod. These dances were all pleasing to the flesh. Therefore, the church must not assume that all dances are acceptable. If the dance movements—whether it is in the dance ministry or congregation during praise and worship—do not glorify God, they are not pleasing to God.

This is very important for the praise dancer. During the preparation of a dance, the praise dancer must be in the presence of God. One movement inspired by God can deliver a person from bondage. So don't go to the world to get your choreography. Seek God and ask Him what He wants. Pray that He uses your body as an instrument of His glory. Take dance lessons from spirit-filled dance instructors, and discipline yourselves to watch praiseworthy dances for inspiration. Always be mindful that what you allow to enter into your spirit will eventually come out through your praise.

2

Praise & Worship

"Praise the Lord. Praise God in his sanctuary: praise him in the firmament of his power. Praise him for his mighty acts; praise him according to his excellent greatness. Praise him with the sound of the trumpet: praise him with the psaltery and harp. Praise him with the timbrel and DANCE: praise him with stringed instruments and organs. Praise him upon the loud sounding cymbals: praise him upon the high sounding cymbals. Let everything that hath breath Praise ye the Lord." (Psalm 150)

Praise and worship is the time during service when everything that has breath is to praise the Lord. It is the time when we invite God's presence into the service. The time when we can enter into the throne room of God and obtain help in our time of need. In *Psalm 150*, David tells us why we are to praise the Lord, how we are to praise the Lord, and what we are to praise the Lord with.

3

For the most part, we do all of these expressions of worship in our church services during praise and worship today. We sing along with the praise and worship leaders. We play our tambourines and maracas, and even blow our whistles along with the musicians. But for some reason, when it comes to dancing, we leave it up to the dance ministry.

The praise dancers, musicians, and praise and worship leaders are called the praise team in most churches. The praise team leads the congregation into praise and worship unto to God. In *II Chronicles 20:21-22*, the musicians, singers, and—I believe—dancers, went before the Lord's army in battle with praises. When they began to sing and praise the Lord, the Bible said the Lord set up ambushes against the enemy and they were killed. You see, when we assemble in our sanctuaries, the principalities of the air (Satan and his demons) are assembled there also. Their assignment is to cause any and every form of distraction known to man. As the praise team praises God, it prepares the way for God to destroy the enemy and give victory to His people.

God was not speaking to the dance ministry only when He said "praise Him with the dance." He expects all of us to participate. It's a commandment. Some churches have congregational dancing during praise and worship. Congregational dance is when all of the people are dancing harmoniously, doing the same dance movements before God. I look forward to the day when all congregations dance harmoniously before the Lord. I'm not saying that everyone has to dance skillfully. I am saying get involved! There's nothing like the freedom you experience when you dance before the Lord.

I once knew a pastor who quoted *Psalms 118:24* before every service: "This is the day that the Lord has made; let us rejoice and be glad in it." I can't think of a more appropriate way to begin praise and worship than with that scripture. Praise means to glorify and commend God for His attributes. Worship means to offer reverence, admiration, and honor toward God. Rejoice means to be glad, happy, delighted, to be full of joy. It can be expressed as clapping, singing, and dancing, since dance is one of the expressions of rejoicing. I went through the scripture and replaced the word "rejoice" with "dance." My favorite is *Philippians 4:4*, "Rejoice in the Lord always and again I say rejoice." Replace "rejoice" with "dance" and it reads: *Dance in the Lord always and again I say dance.* This tells me that there is always a reason to dance and it's not only when I feel like it, but that I should dance in the good times and in the bad times.

God is clear in the scriptures concerning the dance. He said "Praise Me with the Dance!" So, let us come together and dance corporately before Him. Let us start dancing from the pulpit to the last pew in the sanctuary. Let the aisles be filled with saints dancing unto God. Once we get the revelation and knowledge of this and start putting it to practice, there are going to be breakthroughs throughout the body of Christ like we've never seen before. Glory to God!

Welcoming

"And Jephthah came to Mizpeh unto his house, and behold, his daughter came to meet him with timbrels and with DANCES..." (Judges 11:34)

A welcome dance tells a person that you have been expecting them. It's a wonderful way of saying hello. In some countries, you are greeted at the airport with dancing. My husband and I were greeted with dancing when we arrived in Jamaica. It was something we will never forget. It made us feel important.

This is what I believe God wants us to do when the man or woman of God comes to minister at our churches. The dance ministry should lead the congregation in a welcome dance. Jesus was welcomed by the Jews in *John 12:12-13* when he came to Jerusalem. They waved branches of palm trees and welcomed the King who came in the name of the Lord.

When guest ministers come to our churches, they do not come of themselves, they come in the name of the Lord to preach the Good News. In *Romans 10:15,* Paul said "How beautiful are the feet of them that preach the gospel of peace and bring glad tidings of good things!" It is only fit to welcome them with a celebration. Some of them may have had to press through difficult situations to get to you. Your celebrating them in the dance will lift their spirits.

When we have guest ministers at our church, we bring out the best. We have the dancers, singers, musicians, step ministry and sometimes, popular gospel artists are invited to minister. Our pastors always have us stand to our feet and welcome our guests as they come to minister. God wants us to honor one another and treat each other like royalty. Let the guest ministers know that their labor is not in vain and that you appreciate them. I am sure this type of welcome will outweigh any amount of monetary gift they could ever receive. Give God some praise! Hallelujah!

A Celebration

"Now his elder son was in the field: and as he came and drew nigh to the house, he heard musick and DANCING." (Luke 15:25)

A celebration is held to observe a notable occasion with festivities. We are all familiar with the parable of the prodigal son. A very wealthy father had granted his youngest son's request to receive his inheritance early and travel the world independently. You may recall the son strayed away and spent all of his inheritance on loose living. When the prodigal son returned poor and brokenhearted, he was filthy and covered in rags. His father received him with open arms and gave him the best robe and fed him the best calf. The music and dancing that the elder son heard in the field that day was coming from his father's house. The entire household was celebrating the return of the wayward son.

Are you in a backsliding state and think that you are too filthy to return to God? Do you feel the world has beaten you so badly that you're not fit for the kingdom anymore? God said in *Hosea 14:4* that He will heal your backsliding and will love you freely; for His anger is turned away from you. Nobody is mad at your return but the devil!

In the book of Zephaniah Israel strayed from God and started worshipping other gods. In chapter 3, God restores Israel to himself and rejoices at their return.

Murray Silberling in his book, *"Dancing for Joy,"* said this regarding the term "he will joy" in *Zephaniah 3:17*. "The word that is translated "he will joy" is the term yagil. The literal translation then would be that God dances with joy over us!" I love it, God dancing ! Some of you may have turned from God and are worshipping other gods such as your job, riches, or people. You may feel that the last thing you deserve is for God to dance over you in joy at your return. The truth is, we all deserve death, but God has other plans for us. In *Jeremiah 29:11,* He said He knows the thoughts that He thinks toward us, thoughts of peace and not evil, to give us an expected end. You see, He has already worked it out. So, be assured that God has forgiven you. He is no longer angry. Remember that He is awaiting your return with open arms, ready to give you His best! Dance in celebration of your return, and while you're dancing, He too is dancing over you in heaven. Glory to God!

The Deliverer

"Miriam the prophetess, the sister of Aaron, took a timbrel in her hand; and all the women went out after her with timbrels and with DANCES." (Exodus 15:20)

*O*ne of my favorite times to dance before the Lord is when He has delivered me from the hand of the enemy. In *Exodus chapter 15,* after God closed the Red Sea on Pharaoh's army, Miriam grabbed her timbrel (tambourine) and danced dances of deliverance to God. The other women followed her. I call these women the Miriam Dancers. They danced and sang "I will sing unto the Lord for he has triumphed gloriously; the horse and rider into the sea." I am sure that was a powerful dance. They had not only witnessed God's miraculous power in saving their lives, but they were delivered out of hundreds of years of bondage and oppression. This was also a dance that expressed great gratitude and thanksgiving.

I can think of many times my God has come through and caused triumph in my life. What a mighty God we serve! He has moved obstacles, people, traps, and other hindrances that have come against me. There were many times when He has left my enemies scratching their heads. He delivered me so gloriously that I could not take the credit for myself. No one would have believed me anyway. He not only delivered me, but He delivered me with honor. I looked good when I came out. If you didn't know me personally and what I was going through, you couldn't tell I was in battle! Hallelujah! Isn't that just like God?

You see, your deliverance is not only for you, it's for God's glory. God will deliver you with honor. Isn't that something for you to dance about? Just the thought of where you could be if God had not been on your side should make you leap for joy! He is the Deliverer and our Keeper! He will make a way out of no way every time, if you praise Him like you believe it.

Our Warrior

" … DANCE …to execute vengeance upon the heathen, and punishments upon the people; To bind their kings with chains, and their nobles in fetters of iron; To execute upon them the judgment written: this honour have all his saints." *(Psalms 149:7-8)*

This scripture speaks of spiritual warfare. Warfare means to destroy the works of the enemy. We have the honor of binding the enemy and his demons through the dance. Praise the Lord! Hallelujah! That's good news for me! The devil attacks us in many ways, some harder than others. It is up to us to use all of the tools that God has given us.

Dance is a tool used in warfare. It confuses the devil. In the spirit realm, you are binding him and his demons with chains when you dance. If you're going to engage in this

14

warfare, you must be prepared. The devil wants your joy and your peace. He knows that if he's able to rob you of those two things, you will become discouraged and begin to entertain thoughts of doubt and defeat.

There are times when I've found myself engaged in warfare in the late hours of the night. I may have experienced a day full of obstacles, and when I lie down to rest, the enemy would start to harass me with negative thoughts that would cause me to become anxious and restless. I would do as *II Corinthians 10:5* says and cast down each thought as it came by declaring God's word through scriptures. As soon as I'd cast down one thought, another would follow. I have literally gotten up in the pitch dark, gone to the middle of my bedroom floor, and started to dance. I know it was warfare dance because the movements were sharp and direct. They included stomping, kicking, marching, and the pulling down of strongholds. The movements came as simultaneously as the thoughts. I believe they were pre-planned by God Himself. I would dance until I felt anxiety lift from me. By the time I finished, the thoughts would cease, and my mind would be at perfect peace. I would be exhausted as if I had just finished fighting. I'd lie back down and have the best night's sleep. Glory to God!

This might sound foolish to you or you might be saying to yourselves, "It doesn't take all of that." Yes, it does. The devil comes to kill, to steal, and to destroy us. I don't know about you, but I know who I am in Christ and the Bible tells me that I am more than a conqueror through Christ Jesus! I can't be defeated! Hallelujah!

In *Psalms 24:8,* we are asked the question, "Who is the King of Glory?" The answer follows immediately: "The Lord, strong and mighty in battle is He." He is our Great Warrior! Although God ultimately wins all of our battles for us, He needs us to take some action. We are the army of the Lord and we wrestle not against flesh and blood, but against principalities and powers, against the rulers of the darkness of this world, against spiritual wickedness in high places *(Ephesians 6:12)*. When in battle, we must be ready to use everything we know. Use the word of God as a two-edged sword and the dance to bind the enemy with the chains with which he tried to bind you. We are more than conquerors in the Lord Christ Jesus. God has given us the tools, so let's use them. Praise God!

Mourning into Dancing

"Thou hast turned for me my mourning into DANCING: thou hast put off my sackcloth and girded me with gladness." *(Psalms 30:11)*

"A time to weep, and a time to laugh, a time mourn, a time to DANCE." (Ecclesiastes 3:4)

" 'Then shall the virgin rejoice in the DANCE, both young men and old together: for I will turn their mourning into joy, and will comfort them, and make them rejoice from their sorrow." (Jeremiah 31:13)

*Y*es, we are to mourn, but it's only for a time. Mourning is an expression of sorrow. Usually we mourn when we've lost someone or something dear to us. For most of us, it can be a time of devastation. God wants to turn our mourning into rejoicing (dancing). He wants us to live in joy, not sorrow. Jesus came that our joy may be full. Mourning and sorrow can cause your body to go through physical changes. Not only can it open the door for sickness, it can make you feel isolated from familiar places and people, especially people who are happy.

Are you mourning today or full of sorrow? Just as God did for David, He is able to turn your mourning into dancing and gird (surround) you with gladness. He also said in *Jeremiah 31:13* that He will make you rejoice from your sorrow. This is a great place to replace the word "rejoice" with "dance." *He will make you dance from your sorrow.* Hallelujah!

When you're dancing in mourning and sorrow, God literally pours the oil of joy on you from heaven. The joy of the Lord is your strength—the strength that enables you to face the circumstances of life, however painful they may be.

Dancing in mourning and sorrow declares to the devil that he will not disable you from being effective in the kingdom of God. It releases the tensions of stress and lifts the weights that we so often carry in our lives. God needs our bodies to fulfill His purpose for the world. That is, to win souls for the kingdom. We don't have time to wallow in our sorrows or try to figure out what we could have done to make things different. We need to find strength when we are weak and joy when we are sad. Dancing is one of the ways that God has given us to do this.

Demonic forces are sent to us by Satan in packages of depression, oppression, failure, or disappointment, all designed to make us give up the good fight of faith. When we dance before God, we are showing Him that we are not looking at what we presently see or feel, but that we are standing on His promises. It keeps us encouraged and hopeful during our dark moments. In return, God pours the oil of joy and gladness on us and we find ourselves able to face another day.

Both my parents are deceased, and they both died young. My father was forty-six and my mother was forty-eight. At the time of my mother's death, I was living in Berlin, Germany. On the plane while returning to Germany, I became overwhelmed with sorrow. I cried on and off during the entire nine-hour flight. That night, in my living room, I began to dance before the Lord. I danced every night for almost three weeks. I needed relief from the pain and I believed with all of my heart that if I praised God in the dance, He would make me rejoice from my sorrow. The more I danced, the more I felt the joy of the Lord become my strength. God turned my mourning into dancing! He assured me that my parents were with Him. *I Corinthians 5:3* tells us "to be absent from the body is to be present with the Lord." Both my parents were saved, and I know I will see them again in glory, and for me, that's something to rejoice about.

Another time of sorrow in my life was during the time of believing God for a husband. I listened to tapes on how to have a successful marriage, and attended marriage seminars faithfully. I was determined to do it right the second time around. When I met Robert Wright, I was confident that one thing would lead to another and eventually we were going to be married. However, there came a time during our dating period when we separated and it looked like it was over between us. I wasn't prepared for that, and it was extremely painful.

Despite the fact that my heart was hurting and that I felt like crawling into a hole, I would dance in the aisles of my church during praise and worship before the One who is able to heal the brokenhearted, all the while thanking Him for His promise of healing. He not only healed me, but one year later, I married my Mr. Wright. Hallelujah!

You see, God wants to see if we'll praise Him even when it looks hopeless, even when it hurts. If you believe that He is able to turn your mourning into dancing and your sorrow into rejoicing; if you believe that He is no respecter of persons, *(Acts 10:36)* and if He did it for one, He can do it for you, then dance before Him and give Him all of the glory!

Dancing With Abandonment

"And David DANCED before the Lord with all his might..."
(II Sam. 6:14)

*H*ave you ever had something and lost it as a result of disobedience? When it was restored, did it not bring joy to your soul? Especially when you knew you did nothing to deserve it, but God's mercy allowed you to have it again? We are familiar with the famous dance that David did before the Lord when the Ark of the Covenant was brought into the City of David. David was experiencing restoration. He and 30,000 men were bringing the Ark to the city, when one of the men carrying the Ark touched it with his hand out of disobedience. This angered God and He killed the man on the spot. David was displeased by this and became afraid of the Lord. He left the Ark at the house of Obed-edom.

As the Ark sat there for three months God blessed Obed-edom and his household. When David learned of this, he decided to go and get the Ark. I guess he realized that God was still in the blessing business! The Bible said he brought the Ark of God into the City of David with gladness, accompanied by the House of Israel. They shouted, played their instruments, and had a praise and worship service outside in the streets. David danced before the Lord with abandonment. I assume he danced out of the linen ephod that he was wearing, because his wife Michal was upset about how he uncovered himself before the eyes of the handmaids. Now that's what I call dancing! I see why he was called a man after God's own heart. He knew how to praise Him. His dancing didn't offend the handmaids. They understood that David was worshipping God. Nevertheless, it offended Michal and her reaction caused her to be childless unto death.

Abandonment implies unrestrained freedom of action or emotion. Dancing with abandonment means to dance freely without caring who's watching you or what people are thinking or saying about you. David wasn't caught up in the fact that he was King of Israel. He did not let man define for him how he should praise his God. He danced freely before God without the concern of what people thought. So, if you have to dance out of that sports jacket or out of those shoes that hurt your feet in order to dance freely before the

Lord, do it as unto the Lord, because He deserves all of the praise!

In this chapter, we see that dance is not just for the women of the church. Have you ever seen a man dance before the Lord? It brings joy to my soul watching them put self and ego aside to worship the King of Kings and Lord of Lords. More men need to become unashamed and start dancing for victories in their households. In *Matthew 12:29*, Jesus is speaking when he said "… how can one [speaking of the devil] enter into a strong man's house, and spoil his goods, except he first bind the strong man? And then he will spoil his house." If the devil binds the man, then he spoils the people in his household. When a man dances unashamed before the Lord, the enemy is bound and no weapon formed against him or his household will prosper. Hallelujah!

My husband is six-foot-one and 275 pounds and he dances before the Lord. It took him some getting used to at first. He started one evening in our living room and he has been praising God in the dance ever since. There have been many times when we've needed God to intervene on our behalf in a situation. We would get into the aisles of the church and praise the Lord in the dance. God has been so good to us through the years. We can't imagine worship without dancing. I can relate to how David felt when he said to Michal after she criticized the way he danced before the

Lord in *II Samuel 6:22*. "After all the things that God has done for me, I will dance even more vile than this!" In other words, if you think this was bad, you ain't seen nothing yet!

Webster's Dictionary defines vile as offensive to the senses or sensibilities. I love it! Some will never accept dance as part of worship. Anything you do will be offensive to them. To those of us who have experienced the joys and victories that come from dancing before the Lord, we are always reminded of the words to a song that goes: "When I think of His goodness and what He's done for me, when I think of His goodness and how He set me free, I can DANCE, DANCE, DANCE, DANCE, DANCE, DANCE, DANCE all night!" Hallelujah! He is a faithful God! He said that He inhabits the praises of His people! Try it. Before you know it, you too will be dancing with abandonment before our Father. Glory!

Dancing Prophetically

"And it came to pass as they came, when David was returned from the slaughter of the Philistine, that the women came out of the cities of Israel, singing and DANCING, to meet King Saul with tabrets, with joy, and with instruments of musick And the women answered one another as they played, and said, Saul hath slain his thousands, and David his ten thousands." (I Samuel 18:6-7)

Have you ever heard a prophecy come forth through a song? Well, prophecy also comes forth through the dance. The dance in the above scripture is a Prophetic Dance. Prophecy is the prediction of something to come, inspired by the Spirit of God. It is God giving us a glimpse of the future. The women in *I Samuel 18:6-7* were praising God in advance for what He was going to do. They believed God to the extent that they went out to meet the King (Saul) with a prophecy, that I'm sure he wasn't pleased with, nevertheless they proclaimed it and it came to pass.

The gift of prophecy is one of the spiritual gifts that a praise dancer operates in. As a dancer develops and matures in this area, God will give the praise dancer prophetic movements as the prophet brings forth the prophecy during church services. The dancer does not plan this. It is spontaneous expressive movements done by the leading of the Holy Spirit. I do not advise anyone to do this without the permission of the pastor. You must be lead by the Holy Spirit, and God usually confirms it through the pastor and the prophet. We serve a God of order and therefore, all things must be done decently and in order (*I Corinthians 14:40*). Whether it is through music, song, or dance, God is always communicating with His people. He is always looking for ways to show us that He loves us and that our future is in His hands. Let's give God the praise for his tender mercies towards us. Hallelujah!

Hear the Word of the Lord

"Worship Me in the dance as you praise Me. Come out of your comfort zones and give Me your all. I created you to praise Me with every fiber of your being. I love the praises of my people. Your victory is in your praise.

Not your restricted praise, but your unrestricted praise. Unrestricted praise is what I desire. In the midst of your praises, I <u>will</u> bind the enemy and I <u>will</u> set you free of the bondages in your life. So dance, my children, dance before the Lord your God with all your might" Amen.

Assignment

"And they overcame him (Satan) by the blood of the Lamb (Jesus), and by the word of their testimony ..."(Revelation 12:11)

*N*ow it is time for you to put into action what you have read. Use the following blank pages to write down the areas in your life where you need to put dance. Start to praise God in the dance concerning these areas and watch the Lord of the dance bring you out victoriously everytime. Then, record the victories as a reminder to the devil that you are A OVERCOMER!

To God Be All The Glory

Contact Regina S. Wright at
Marvelous Dance Ministries
P.O. Box 1371 Wheaton, MD. 20915
marvelousdance@verizon.net

Bibliography

Silberling, Murray. *Dancing for Joy*. Baltimore, Maryland: Messianic Jewish Publishers, 1995.

Webster's New World Dictionary, Third College Edition. Cleveland, Ohio: Webster's New World Dictionaries. 1991

Scripture quotations are from the King James Version of the Bible.

CPSIA information can be obtained at www.ICGtesting.com
Printed in the USA
LVOW13s2144060813

346673LV00001B/33/A